Every Kid's Guide to
The Juvenile Justice System

Written by
JOY BERRY

CHILDRENS PRESS ®
CHICAGO

About the Author and Publisher

Joy Berry's mission in life is to help families cope with everyday problems and to help children become competent, responsible, happy individuals. To achieve her goal, she has written over two hundred self-help books for children from infancy through age twelve. Her work has revolutionized children's publishing by providing families with practical, how-to, living skills information that was previously unavailable in children's books.

Joy has gathered a dedicated team of experts, including psychologists, educators, child developmentalists, writers, editors, designers, and artists to form her publishing company and to help produce her work.

The company, Living Skills Press, produces thoroughly researched books and audiovisual materials that successfully combine humor and education to teach children subjects ranging from how to clean a bedroom to how to resolve problems and get along with other people.

Managing Editor: Ellen Klarberg
Copy Editors: Kate Dickey, Annette Gooch
Contributing Editors: Jean Buckley, Nancy Cochran, Barbara Detrich,
Frank Elia, Bob Gillen, Kathleen McBride,
Susan Motycka, Gary Passarino
Editorial Assistant: Sandy Passarino

Art Director: Laurie Westdahl
Design: Abigail Johnston, Laurie Westdahl
Production: Abigail Johnston, Caroline Rennard
Illustrations designed by: Bartholomew
Inker: Susie Hornig
Colorer: Susie Hornig
Composition: Curt Chelin

Have you ever wondered what would happen to you if you broke the law?

In **EVERY KID'S GUIDE TO THE JUVENILE JUSTICE SYSTEM,** you will learn the following:

- what happens if you break the law,
- what happens if you are cited,
- what happens if you are booked,
- what happens at an arraignment,
- what happens at a dispositional hearing, and
- what happens if you are made a ward of the court.

A *minor,* depending on the state in which he or she lives, is a person who is under the age of 18 or 21. A minor is often called a *juvenile.* A minor who breaks the law is often called a *juvenile delinquent.* Juvenile delinquents are treated differently from adults who break the law.

Juvenile delinquents are under the jurisdiction of the *juvenile justice system.* This system provides places to stay for children (places such as Juvenile Hall or foster homes) who have been found guilty of crimes or who cannot live with their parents. It provides special courts (juvenile courts) where cases concerning juveniles can be heard by a judge. The juvenile justice system also provides probation officers to guide and oversee the juveniles in their care.

Here is what will happen to you if you are accused of breaking the law.

First, there will be a *police investigation.* This means that a police officer will look into what has happened and decide whether he or she believes that you have disobeyed the law. If the police officer believes that you have disobeyed the law, he or she can do one of three things:
- reprimand and release you,
- cite you, or
- book you.

Sometimes a police officer might *reprimand* you (tell you that you have done something that is against the law) and then give you a *warning* (tell you what will happen to you if you do the same thing again).

After reprimanding and warning you, the police officer might *release* you (let you go).

Sometimes a police officer might *cite* you. This means that he or she may give you a *citation*, which is a summons (ticket) requiring you to report to a probation officer on a certain day.

Sometimes, after you have done something that is against the law, you might be **arrested** (held or detained by a police officer) and **taken into custody** (forced to go with a police officer).

If you are arrested, the law requires the police officer who arrests you to tell you what your rights are.

This is what the police officer is required to tell you:

After you have been arrested and taken into custody, the police officer will take you to *Juvenile Hall* (Juvenile Hall is a place where you stay until a probation officer or the court decides what should happen to you). There you will be **booked.** This means that your name and other information about you, along with an account of your arrest and the date it occurred, are written in Juvenile Hall records.

If you are cited, you will report to a *probation officer.*

A probation officer is someone who will
- help decide whether the court should become involved in your case,
- help the court decide whether you are innocent or guilty, and
- supervise you by making sure that you do what you are supposed to do.

The probation officer can decide to do one of three things. He or she can
- reprimand and release you,
- put you on informal probation, or
- file a petition against you.

If the probation officer decides to *reprimand* and *release* you, all is forgiven and you can go without suffering any consequences.

If the probation officer decides to put you on *informal probation,* you must promise that you will not break the law again, and your parents must agree to help you keep your promise. While you are on informal probation, you might be required to see the probation officer a few times so that he or she can make sure you are staying out of trouble and doing what you are supposed to do.

If the probation officer decides to *file a petition against you,* things can get pretty complicated. Generally speaking, this will not happen if you have been cited. It usually happens only if a person has been booked, so let's move on to "booking." We will talk about filing a petition later.

When you are booked, you will be held at Juvenile Hall. Your parents will be notified as soon as possible. They will be told of your arrest and where you are being held.

At Juvenile Hall you will be assigned to a probation officer. The probation officer at Juvenile Hall can either
- reprimand and release you,
- put you on informal probation, or
- file a petition against you.

The probation officer must decide if he or she is going to file a petition against you within 48 hours (not including weekends and holidays) after your arrest.

If the probation officer decides to file a petition against you, you will have a *detention hearing* within 24 hours after the petition has been filed. During those 24 hours the probation officer might release you, but *only if*

- you are not a danger to yourself or others,
- you are not likely to run away,
- you are not already on probation because of a past offense, and
- you do not come from an unfit home (where there is no one to take care of you).

The detention hearing will take place in a *juvenile court* (a court where people 18 years old and under are tried). You, your parents, and your lawyer must be there. A juvenile court judge or referee will be in charge. He or she is the person who will help decide where you should stay while you are waiting for your arraignment.

Each time you go to court you must have a *lawyer* go with you. It will be the lawyer's job to *defend* you. This means that he or she will make sure the court hears your side of the story. The lawyer will also do everything possible to see that you are treated fairly.

There are two ways you can get a lawyer:
- Your parents can hire one.
- The court can assign you one.

Hiring a lawyer can be very expensive. Because many people cannot afford to do this, there are *public defenders.* A public defender is hired by the public to defend people. If your parents do not hire a lawyer for you, it is most likely that the judge will assign your case to a public defender.

At the detention hearing, the judge or referee
will usually decide that you must

- live at home and have your parents be
  responsible for you,
- live at home and have a probation officer be
  responsible for you, or
- stay in Juvenile Hall.

You will then wait for your *arraignment*. An
arraignment is a court appearance advising
people of the charges against them.

When the probation officer *files a petition* against you, he or she gives a report to the district attorney. The district attorney is the person who tries to have people convicted for the offenses they have been accused of.

The report the probation officer gives the
district attorney includes the police report and
the charges against you, which are the things you
have been accused of.

If the district attorney approves the petition, he or she files the petition with the court. This means that he or she writes up the information in the probation officer's report and gives it to the court.

The district attorney also sets the court date. This means that he or she works with the court to set up a time for you to go to court.

After the district attorney files the petition, you must go to juvenile court again. Your parents and your lawyer must go with you to the arraignment. At court the judge will read the charges that have been filed against you by the district attorney.

After the judge reads the district attorney's report, you will have a chance to tell your side of the story.

At the arraignment one of three things may happen:

- You will be *dismissed.*
- You will *plead guilty as charged.*
- You will *plead not guilty as charged.*

If, after hearing both sides of the story, the judge believes that you are *innocent* (you did not do the things you were accused of doing), he or she can *dismiss the charges.* This means that he or she lets you go without having to suffer any consequences for the offenses you have been accused of.

When you tell the judge your side of the story, you can plead *guilty* or *not guilty*.

If you plead guilty, you admit that you did the things that you have been accused of.

If you plead guilty, the judge will ask a probation officer to look into your situation and recommend what should be done with you. Then you will be told to come back to court for a *dispositional hearing.*

If you plead not guilty, you are saying that you did not do the things you have been accused of.

If you plead not guilty, the judge will have you come back to court for a *trial.*

BECAUSE THE DISTRICT ATTORNEY SAYS THAT YOU ARE GUILTY AND YOU SAY THAT YOU ARE NOT, YOU MUST COME BACK TO COURT FOR A TRIAL. AT THE TRIAL IT WILL BE DECIDED WHETHER YOU ARE GUILTY OR NOT GUILTY.

The trial is always held in juvenile court. At the trial the judge will listen to all the *evidence* for and against you. The evidence is the *proof* people present to show that what they say is true.

After hearing all the evidence, the judge will decide whether you are guilty or not guilty. If the judge decides that you are not guilty, he or she will dismiss the charges and let you go. If the judge decides that you are guilty, he or she will ask a probation officer to look into your situation and recommend what should be done with you. Then you will be told to come back to court for a dispositional hearing.

At the dispositional hearing, the probation officer will talk about your situation and recommend to the judge what should happen to you. The district attorney may also make recommendations. The judge listens to all the recommendations and then decides what should be done.

Most of the time the judge will follow the recommendations of the probation officer, but sometimes he or she will follow the recommendations of the district attorney.

After the judge decides what should be done, he or she will *sentence* you. This means that he or she will tell you what consequences you will suffer for breaking the law. Your sentence will include *where* you will stay, *how long*, and *what* you must do while you are there.

The judge might put you on *six months' probation.* If this happens, you must follow *court orders* (the rules made by the court) for six months. A probation officer will keep in touch with you to make sure you obey the court orders. He or she may also come up with additional rules you must follow while you are on probation.

If you are placed on six months' probation, your parents still have custody of you (this means they are responsible for you) and you will usually live at home.

The judge might make you a *ward of the court.* If this happens, the court will put a probation officer in charge of you. The probation officer will see that you are cared for and kept out of trouble. However, if you are made a ward of the court, your case will be reviewed by the court at least once a year to decide whether you should remain a ward of the court.

There are several places you can stay while you are a ward of the court.

Home. You can stay at your home, but the probation officer is responsible for you, and you must cooperate fully with him or her.

A foster home. This is a home-away-from-home where a foster parent, an adult licensed by the state, takes care of a child with special needs. In most cases a child lives in a foster home that is in his or her community. The foster parent helps care for a child, but the probation officer is responsible for him or her.

A group home. This is a place for children who cannot stay in their own homes or in foster homes. Usually, there are about six children living together in a group home, and there is constant adult supervision. Children in a group home usually attend a public school. In addition, each child reports to a probation officer who is responsible for him or her. Although a group home is privately owned, it is licensed by the state to make sure the children are treated fairly and cared for responsibly.

A private institution. A private institution is similar to a group home in that it is privately owned and licensed by the state. It is usually larger than a group home, and the children are more confined.

A camp. A camp is owned and run by the county. Most camps have a highly organized program that often includes a school. The children go to the school provided by the camp rather than to a public school. Children who live in camps also report to probation officers who are responsible for them.

Juvenile Hall. Juvenile Hall is a place for children who continue to violate the law after spending time in a foster home, group home, institution, or camp. It is also a place where children are sometimes booked and held until they go to court. Children who are sent to Juvenile Hall are carefully supervised and kept in "secure confinement." They must also continue to report to their probation officers.

The state correctional institution. Children are sent to a state correctional institution when they
- have committed very serious crimes;
- cannot be contained or controlled by programs offered through the county (such as foster homes, group homes, private institutions, camps, or Juvenile Hall); or
- have special needs that cannot be met by the county.

Children in state correctional institutions are constantly supervised and kept in "maximum confinement."

IN OTHER WORDS, A STATE CORRECTIONAL INSTITUTION IS **NOT** THE PLACE TO BE.

All of this is to say that breaking the law is a very serious action. It can cause you to suffer some pretty uncomfortable consequences. This is why it is important to find out about the laws that you must obey and then...